WHAT DO YOU Know!

TECH-KNOWLEDGE

ROBOTICS, SPACE EXPLORATION, TANKS

Lynn Peppas and Sonya Newland

A Crabtree Canopy Book

Crabtree Publishing

crabtreebooks.com

IMAGE CREDITS

Dreamstime:

Library of Congress:

NASA: p 22; p 25 (bottom); p 29 (inset); p 32 (left); p 33; p 35 (inset); p 37 (bottom); p 38-39;

Public Domain: NASA/Robert Markowitz, p 4 (bottom left); U.S. Air Force photo by Bobbi Zapka, p 14; p 43; Anton Hoffmann (1863-1938), p 48; p 49 (top);

Shutterstock: Everett Collection, p 50-51; Opachevsky Irina, p 55 (top); Karolis Kavolelis, p 57;

Wikimedia Commons: Robert Fuqua, p 9 (top); Petar Milošević, p 9 (bottom); Sgt. Michael J. MacLeod, p 12; p 13; Travelarz, p 17 (left); MIT Museum, p 17 (top); Ralf Roletschek, p 18 (right); Albert van Breemen, p 18 (inset); NASA/MSFC, p 24; AElfwine, p 25 (left); NASA, p 26, 28, 31; Creative Commons, NASA, p 27 (top); U.S. National Archives and Records Administration, pgs 54, 55, 56, 58; New Zealand Defence Force, p 59; p 60; Republic of Korea Armed Forces, p 61

All other images from Shutterstock

Authors: Lynn Peppas, Sonya Newland
Editor: Kathy Middleton
Proofreader: Melissa Boyce
Design: Tammy McGarr
Production manager: Candice Campbell

Crabtree Publishing

crabtreebooks.com 800-387-7650

Printed in the U.S.A./CP2025

Published in Canada
Crabtree Publishing
616 Welland Ave.
St. Catharines, Ontario
L2M 5V6

Published in the United States
Crabtree Publishing
347 Fifth Ave.
Suite 1402-145
New York, NY 10016

Library and Archives Canada Cataloguing in Publication
Available at Library and Archives Canada

Library of Congress Cataloging-in-Publication Data
Available at the Library of Congress

Hardcover: 978-1-0398-9767-0
Ebook (pdf): 978-1-0398-8182-2
Epub: 978-1-0398-8302-4

Contents

CHAPTER 1

ROBOTICS

Robots in History

NASA astronaut Doug Sparks was repairing a faulty part outside the International Space Station (ISS) as it **orbited** Earth more than 230 miles (370 km) away. Suddenly, he felt terrible pain near his stomach. Doug told ISS astronauts inside that he needed help—and fast. They sent the station's robot, Robonaut 2, to get Doug.

Robonaut 2 brought Doug back inside and diagnosed him as having appendicitis. Doug needed emergency surgery or he would die. Robonaut 2 prepared Doug for surgery. A surgical robot, called da Vinci, performed it successfully. Doug's life was saved in space by robots. This story isn't completely true—surgery has not been performed in space yet—but it could be in the very near future!

The surgical robot, da Vinci, was designed in 2000 to perform battlefield surgery from a distance. Today, da Vinci performs surgery (on Earth) with the guidance of human surgeons miles away.

Imagining Robots Long Ago

Almost 3,000 years ago, a Greek poet named Homer imagined what life would be like with robots. In a poem called the *Iliad*, he wrote about female servant robots made of gold. Many centuries later, the famous Italian artist and inventor Leonardo da Vinci designed a **robotic** knight in the late 1400s. Da Vinci's knight could sit, stand, move its head, and lift its face shield.

Da Vinci's invention is called an **automaton**. Between 1768 and 1774, Pierre and Henri-Louis Jaquet-Droz also made automata in the forms of a woman playing a piano, a young child that draws four different pictures, and another that writes up to 40 letters.

In 1948, a tortoise robot created by American inventor William Grey Walter turned what had once only been imagined, one step closer to reality. Walter's tortoise was special because it had **sensors**. It reacted to light and avoided anything in its way. It seemed to think and move on its own.

In 1954, American inventor George Devol was the first to design a robot that could be programmed to do different tasks. About 20 years later, WABOT-1 was created in Tokyo, Japan. WABOT-1 could see, grasp, walk, and speak a few words.

Robots at Work

Some jobs are extremely dangerous and even impossible for humans to do. Others are too disgustingly dirty, or too boring for humans. Twentieth-century robots became the answer to the problem: who will do the work that nobody wants to do?

Raymond Goertz invented the first telerobot in 1951. It was a robotic arm, designed to handle material that was not safe for humans. A telerobot, or teleoperator, is a machine that is remotely controlled, or controlled from a safe distance, by a human. It is sometimes called a "master-slave" robot. The master is the human controlling the robotic arm, or the slave.

The automobile industry uses more robots on assembly lines than any other industry.

A robot's ability to move is called its degrees of freedom (DOF). It is a measurement of the number of twists, turns, or rolls it can do.

Industrial robots repeat the same job over and over again, and never get tired or bored. They can work 24 hours a day and never need breaks, take vacations, or get sick. They work faster and have greater strength than people—and they almost never make mistakes.

But everything wears out in time, and robots do need to be checked to see that they are working properly, or fixed if they break down. Most industrial robots that work on assembly lines are **stationary** and have one or more working arms. In 2023, there were more than 4 million working industrial robots on Earth!

"Hello, Earth Person. Welcome to the Robot Restaurant," the robot says as you enter. Another robot waiter takes your order. Robots in the kitchen cook your order, which the robot waiter then delivers to your table. Dining entertainment includes a robot that sings while you eat.

Although robots do not get sick days off from work, there is the rare time that they may need a few repairs and maintenance.

Robots in Our Lives

Although it might sound like something from the distant future, restaurants staffed with robot workers first opened in China in 2009. Service robots can work for five hours before needing to recharge. Other restaurants around the world have started employing robots for cooking and serving.

KUKA Titan is a heavyweight champion of industrial robots. The robotic stationary arm lifts objects that weigh more than 2,200 pounds (998 kg) effortlessly. Objects such as cars or cement staircases that are usually handled by cranes are no problem for this much smaller, but mightier, industrial arm.

In the past, a dairy cow had to wait for the farmer to milk her. But today, she decides when she will be milked. She walks right into the Lely Astronaut A4 milking robot. While the robot milks her, she eats a treat of some grains. Life is good—even for a cow—with robot helpers.

Robots today greet and serve customers in restaurants, and can even cook the meal!

Farm robots lighten farmers' loads by doing tasks such as harvesting, caring for crops, and milking cows. This automatic milker uses a laser to find the cow's teats and can milk a herd without human help.

Robots in Space

During the 1950s, robots were a popular theme in books and movies. American author Isaac Asimov published a book of sci-fi short stories called *I, Robot* in 1950. Asimov created Three Laws of Robotics in *I, Robot,* which are still referred to today in television shows such as *The Simpsons* and movies such as *I, Robot* (2004).

The Day the Earth Stood Still was a popular movie in 1951. It was about an alien named Klaatu and his robot Gort, who travel to Earth in a spaceship. Over 70 years later, human-designed robots are traveling through space to visit other planets. But, this time, it's for real!

Robots Working in Space

Lunokhod was the first robot on the Moon. The eight-wheeled, robotic **rover** landed on the Moon on November 17, 1970. This hard-working robot traveled more than 6 miles (10 km), took more than 20,000 images, and tested the Moon's soil for 11 months.

The Canadarm is another first for robotics in space. This Canadian-designed robotic arm was first put to work aboard the *Columbia* STS-2 space shuttle on November 13, 1981. Since then, the six-jointed arm has solved a number of problems in space such as breaking dangerous ice off shuttles and repairing the Hubble Space Telescope.

Scientists have long wondered if people could live on Mars. But it is too dangerous and expensive to send astronauts. NASA decided to send the next best thing–robots! Sojourner rover was the first to explore Mars in 1997. Spirit and Opportunity followed in 2004. Curiosity landed in 2012.

> *"[The Canadarm] was like an extension of your own arm. I [loved] how neat it was, how much like the human arm it was.... It was my first exposure to real robotics."*
>
> *Space Shuttle STS-2 Mission commander Joe Engle*

The Canadarm2 grabs and moves heavy objects in space. It has 7 DOF and is over 55 feet (17 m) long.

Future Robots in Space

An insect-like robot flies from the back of a Mars rover. It has twin wings, one fluttering on the front and another on the back. It quickly flies close to the planet's surface. It slows down and hovers over an interesting rock. A small arm extends to take a sample. Drawing the arm back inside its body, it quickly flies back to the rover to bring the rock sample for study and to refuel.

This insect-like robot is called an entomopter. "Entomo" means insect. NASA is working toward designing a more advanced entomopter robot that could fly over difficult areas and through the thin air of the Martian **atmosphere**.

Mars Exploration rovers have special tools that help investigate the surface of Mars. The rock abrasion tool (RAT) can dig into hard rock. A robotic arm and magnets help collect soil samples. The magnets attract and collect magnetic dust found in the air on Mars. Cameras take close-up images of samples. Scientific tools called spectrometers analyze samples to see what they are made of.

Perseverance is about 10 feet (3 m) long and 9 feet (2.7 m) wide—around the size of a small car.

The latest Mars rover, Perseverance, landed on Mars in February 2021. Building on the discoveries of earlier Mars rovers, Perseverance is tasked with looking for evidence of any previous life on the red planet.

Military Robots

American soldiers wait outside a building where they believe enemy soldiers are inside. If they enter, they could be shot, or it could be **booby-trapped** with a bomb. One soldier takes a Packbot 510 from his backpack. He sets up a laptop computer and operates the robot with a videogame controller. Packbot 510 searches the building on **tracks** attached to a belt that rotates around wheels. The Packbot 510 can search for enemy soldiers and explosives.

Packbot 510 is only one of a number of robots that help save lives in the military. Cameras send images back to a soldier's laptop. It is equipped with thermal imaging. Thermal imaging uses the heat that an object or living thing gives off to help them see in the dark. Sensors sniff out bombs, chemical poisons, and **radiation**.

*These **paratroopers** are being trained to use the Packbot.*

Battlefields are one of the most dangerous places to be. Soldiers in combat are fighting for their lives. But what happens if a soldier is shot, injured, and cannot move to safety or get medical attention? Another person coming in to save the injured soldier would also risk getting shot.

The BEAR, created by Vecna, is a disaster recovery robot that could help in this situation. "BEAR" stands for Battlefield Extraction-Assist Robot. The BEAR is designed to locate, lift, and carry a person or other heavy item, without risking other people's lives to do so.

After Japan's earthquake in 2011, Packbot 510 worked inside the damaged nuclear power plant because the leaking radiation was too dangerous for people.

"Packbot fulfilled a mission that flesh-and-bones soldiers, risking life and limb, used to do.... More than 750 such robots have been lost in combat in Iraq and Afghanistan—a number that translates into many saved lives."

The Wall Street Journal, *2012*

You'll probably never see the RQ-4 Global Hawk—not while it's working, anyway. This UAV can fly up to about 11 miles (18 km) high.

The military uses flying UAVs (unmanned aerial vehicles) and UCAVs (unmanned combat aerial vehicles) to keep watch over troubled areas and nations. They are sometimes called drones. Robotic aircraft do **reconnaissance** missions without a person inside the cockpit. Some are even armed to strike enemy targets with missiles in exactly the right spot.

Most UAVs and UCAVs are directed by a pilot at a faraway base, using a remote control. Sensors on the UAV can read a car's license plate from 2 miles (3 km) away! Robotic aircraft can travel through dangerous areas without risk to human life. Some, such as the RQ-4 Global Hawk, can stay in the air for up to 30 hours.

The RQ-4 Global Hawk is one of the most expensive robots on Earth. One Global Hawk costs over $100 million! But most military professionals agree that it's worth every penny for the jobs it can do.

Medical Robots

Pat had cancer. A tumor, or growth, at the base of his tongue had to be removed. It was a risky operation—a human surgeon would have to saw Pat's lower jaw in half to get at the tumor to remove it. Even if the operation went well, Pat would be left with a large scar on his throat and many weeks of painful recovery.

Pat and his doctor decided to use a groundbreaking surgical robot called da Vinci instead. The da Vinci robot's smaller surgical instruments would be able to reach the tumor by going in through Pat's mouth. The instruments would be guided by the human surgeon's hand movements on a controller. The surgery was over in less than half an hour without having to cut through Pat's jawbone.

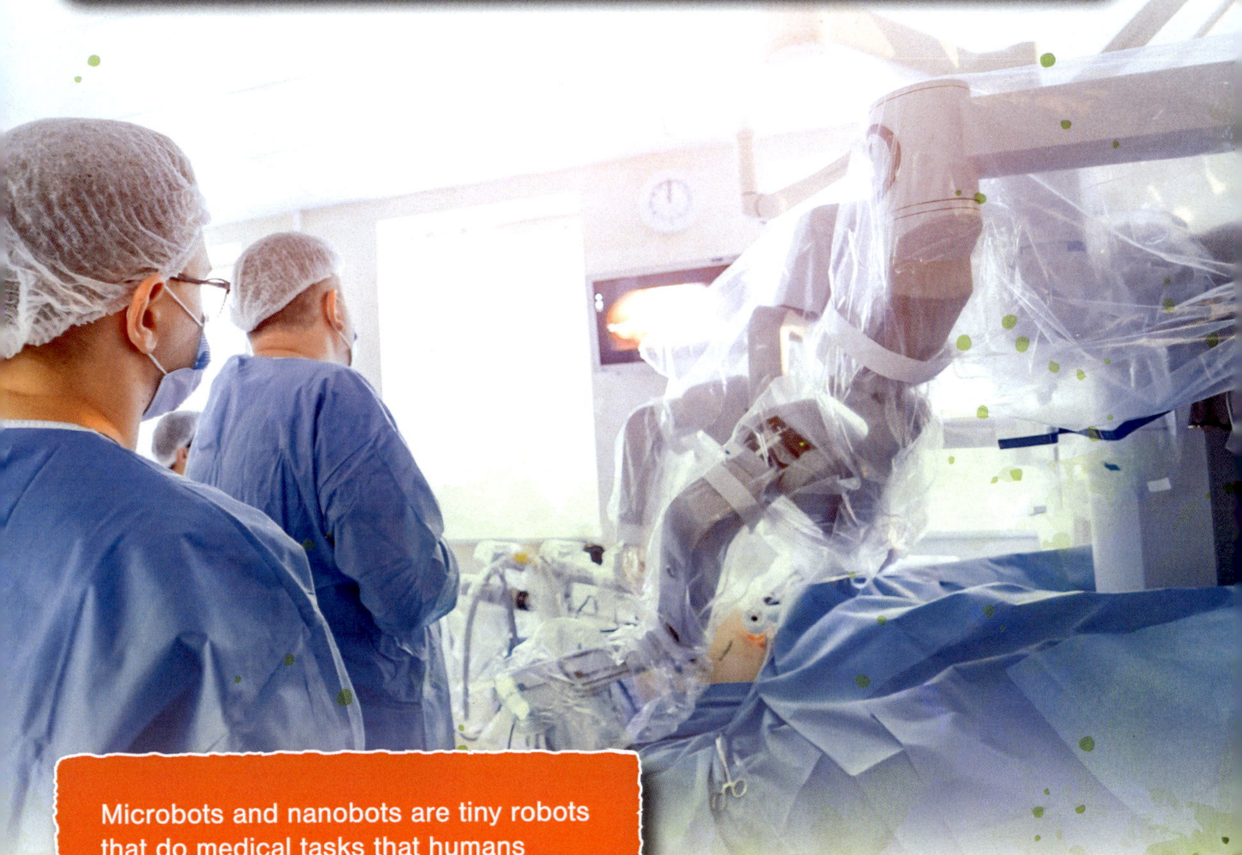

Microbots and nanobots are tiny robots that do medical tasks that humans cannot do. The Norika3 is a robot that a patient swallows. The capsule releases a camera that moves through a person's **digestive system** and takes images.

A surgical robot leaves smaller scars, and means quicker recovery times and shorter hospital stays for patients.

Natalie is an elderly person with a disability. Natalie's relatives worry that something might happen to her while she's home alone, and she won't be able to call for help. They want her to move into a nursing home, but Natalie does not want to go there. Nurse-bots (the short form for nurse-robots) could help.

Nurse-bots are robots that help care for older or disabled people. A nurse-bot can lift a person from their bed into a wheelchair. Nurse-bots can also do tasks such as make meals or carry household items. They can remind people when to take their medicine or when to eat or drink.

Nurse-bots provide their patients with telepresence. Telepresence allows people who are not together to see and communicate with each other by computer screens. Patients could visit with health care providers, relatives, or others through this technology.

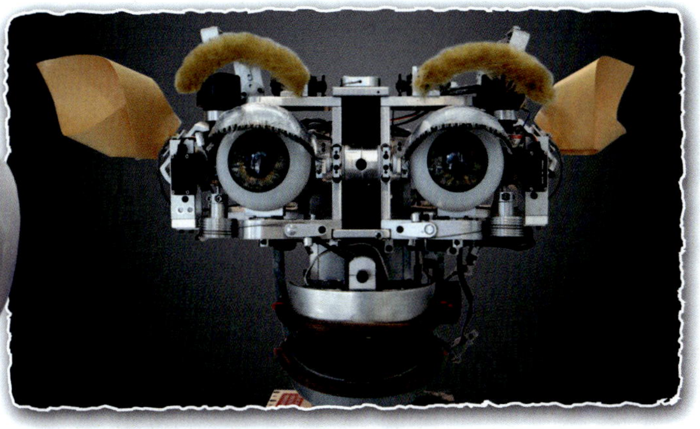

Kismet (shown here) was designed by roboticist professor Cynthia Breazeal in the late 1990s.

Humanoid Robots

"You're adorable," says Cynthia to a robotic head named Kismet. Kismet responds by making a facial expression of happiness like a child. Kismet's facial features (eyes, eyebrows, neck, lips, and ears) each have two or more DOF (see page 6). These allow Kismet to show emotions such as happiness, sadness, disgust, excitement, anger, surprise—just about any emotion a human face can show.

Kismet has what are called robotiquette skills. Robotiquette is the acceptable social rules and behaviors shown by a robot toward a human. Proper robotiquette makes people comfortable interacting with robots.

People relate better to robots that show facial expressions and emotions. On the other hand, robots that are too human-like can make people feel uncomfortable.

Humans vs. Humanoids?

It is the year 2050. Two soccer teams face each other on the field: the World Cup soccer champions vs. the RoboCup soccer champions. One is a team of athletic young men. The other is a team of **humanoid** robots. Who will win? Only time will tell.

The RoboCup is the most famous competition between robots in the world. This robot soccer game is a lot slower-paced than a human soccer game. The robot players on each team are not able to run. They can only walk forward, sideways, and kick the ball. Sometimes they fall over, but they can get up by themselves. But, even in soccer, robotics is quickly improving!

"Robots are made to do special jobs. And what they must be able to do is perform those special tasks a thousand times better than a human so that we benefit."

Hiroaki Kitano, artificial intelligence specialist and founder of RoboCup

The official goal of RoboCup is to design a team of humanoid robot soccer players that will defeat the human World Cup soccer champions by 2050!

Extreme Robots

In 1992, a volcano erupted at Mount Spurr, Alaska. Volcanic craters are one of Earth's most dangerous environments. In the past, scientists collected high-temperature gas samples from volcanoes to study them further. But it is a dangerous job. Eight scientists died in 1993 during two separate events while sampling volcanoes. A team from NASA designed a robot called Dante II that would measure dangerous volcanic activity instead of sending a human to do the job.

In 1994, it took Dante II over three days to reach the floor of the volcanic crater on its eight crab-like legs. Information gathered from Dante's sensors and cameras were sent to scientists 50 miles (80 km) away from the crater.

Dante II's exploration of a volcanic crater included traveling along steep walls to the volcano floor. Scientists used Dante II's journey to research how to build other robots to explore other planets in the future.

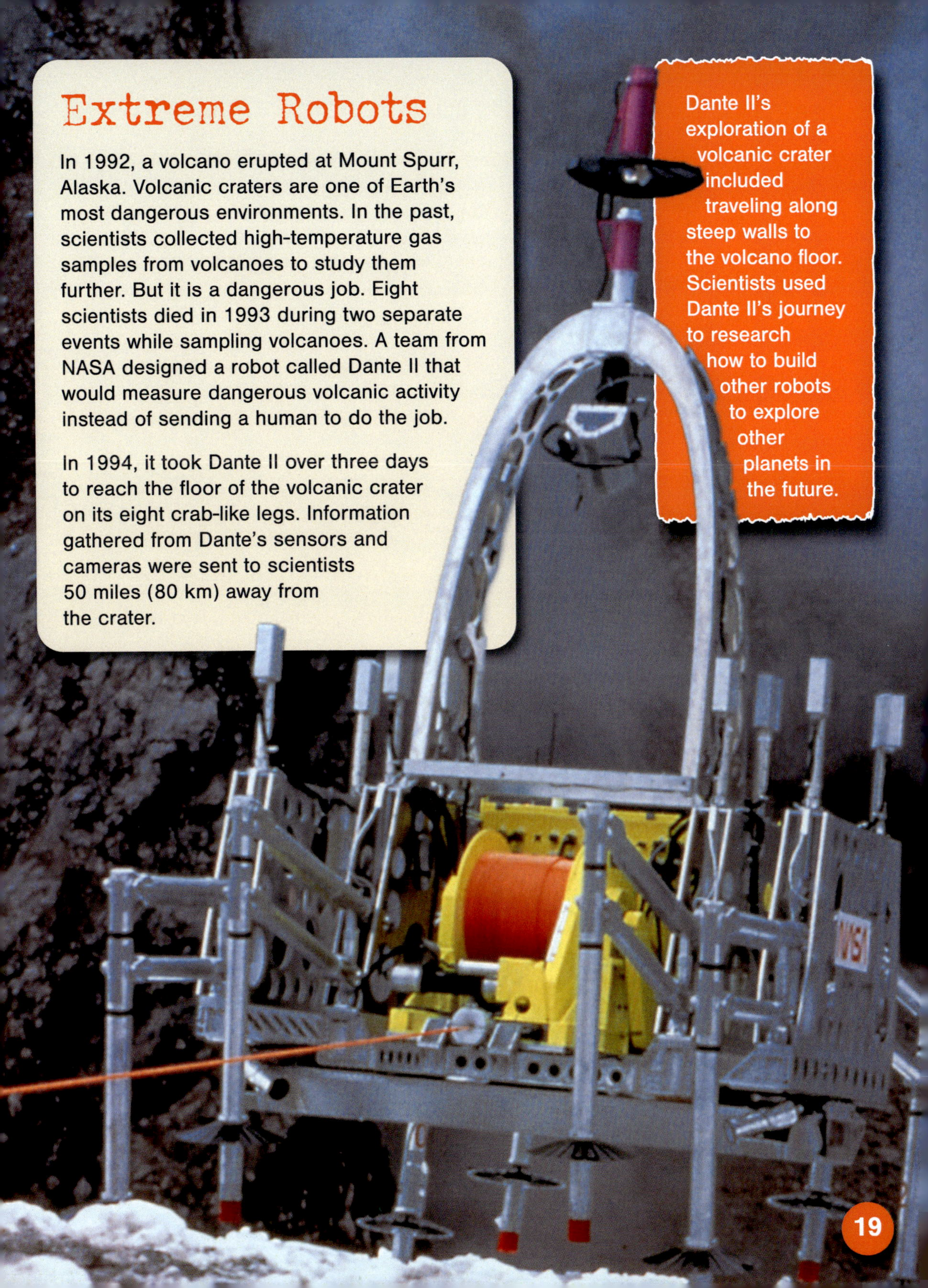

Underwater Robots

Air France Flight 447 tragically crashed into the Atlantic Ocean off South America in 2009. Its whereabouts remained a mystery for about two years. In 2011, an AUV (**autonomous** underwater vehicle) spotted and photographed AF Flight 447's wreckage located more than 2 miles (3 km) underwater. Humans cannot withstand the pressure underwater at the depths that robots can.

Another robotic submarine called the Remora 6000 was sent down to find the plane's flight data recorder, called the black box. Using its two arms and color cameras, the Remora 6000 was able to recover the black box and help solve the mystery of why the plane went down. The plane was going too slowly, stalled in the air, and fell into the ocean.

A remotely operated vehicle (ROV) hangs on the Launch & Recovery System (LARS). The ROV will perform an underwater pipeline survey and inspection.

Robots in the Future

In 2004, a World Robot Declaration statement was released. It stated that: "Next-generation robots will be partners that **coexist** with human beings.... Next-generation robots will contribute to the realization of a safe and peaceful society."

Scientists are already working on nanobots that are even more advanced. Others are working on robotic parts that can replace human limbs and other body parts. Robotic technology is always advancing. Who knows what robots will be capable of doing for humans in the future?

Timeline

1948	William Grey Walter invents a robotic tortoise with sensors
1954	George Devol designs the first robot that could be programmed to do different tasks
November 17, 1970	The first robotic rover, Lunokhod, lands on the Moon
November 13, 1981	The robotic arm, Canadarm, is used on its first space flight
1997	The robotic rover Sojourner explores Mars
2004	The robotic rovers Spirit and Opportunity explore Mars
2011	An AUV discovers Air France Flight 447 at the bottom of the Atlantic Ocean
2012	The robotic rover Curiosity explores Mars
2021	The robotic rover Perseverance explores Mars
2034	The estimated date when most households will be cleaned, managed, and cared for by robots

CHAPTER 2

Space Exploration

Early Exploration

"Houston, we've had a problem here." The voice of astronaut Jack Swigert crackled through to NASA's Mission Control in Texas. **CapCom** Jack Lousma asked Swigert to repeat the message. His fellow astronaut, Commander Jim Lovell, took the radio. "We've had a main B bus undervolt," he reported. Something had gone terribly wrong on board Apollo 13.

Two days into their journey to the Moon, the astronauts were more than 200,000 miles (322,000 km) from Earth. They were running out of air and they no longer had enough electricity to get them home. It was Mission Control's job to bring them back alive.

Mission Control talks to astronaut Fred Haise (on the screen) during the Apollo 13 mission.

Staring into Space

For hundreds of years, humans have looked up at the night sky and asked questions about what they saw. What is the Sun? How many other planets are there? How far away are the stars? Ancient astronomers did not have telescopes or spacecraft to find the answers. Their knowledge of space was based on what they could see with the naked eye.

In ancient times, people set their calendars by the movements of the Sun and Moon. They discovered that objects in space had an effect on the weather and the tides. Tides are the way the sea rises and falls throughout the day. They saw their heroes and gods in the patterns of the stars called constellations.

Astronomy in Ancient Greece

The ancient Greeks began applying math to the movement of objects in space. They discovered that Earth moved around the Sun and that the Moon traveled around Earth. Greek astronomers were the first to realize that Earth must be round. They also worked out what caused **eclipses**.

In 1609, the Italian astronomer Galileo Galilei was the first person to look at the night sky through a telescope. He made many discoveries, including the rings around Saturn and Jupiter's moons. Telescopes showed that there was a lot more to space than anyone had ever imagined. But it was many years later before people had the technology to travel into space.

NASA is the United States' National Aeronautics and Space Administration. It was set up in 1958 to develop technology that would help people learn more about—and travel in—space.

The prehistoric monument Stonehenge, in the UK, may be linked to astronomy. From a certain position, the Heel Stone of Stonehenge lines up with the sunrise in midsummer and sunset in midwinter.

The Space Race

After World War II (1939–1945), the United States and the Soviet Union (USSR) were the most powerful nations on Earth. They each wanted to be the first to send people to space. Both countries put their best scientists to work figuring out how to build machines that could travel beyond Earth.

During the war, scientists had developed rockets to use as weapons. These deadly devices could travel great distances. During a test in 1942, a German V-2 rocket had shot to 60 miles (100 km) above Earth's surface—the very edge of space. Afterward, experts realized they could use rockets like this to launch spacecraft.

German scientist Wernher von Braun helped the Americans develop their rocket technology after the war.

To make a rocket work, gases are shot out of the engine at such high speeds that they power the rocket forward. Spacecraft need to be launched with huge force to help them break free of Earth's **gravity** and reach space.

In 1957, the USSR launched the first **satellite**, which they called Sputnik 1. It spent three months in space—a journey of more than 43 million miles (69 million km). This small metal ball was the first human-made object to circle Earth in space. The event marked the start of a period of time known as the "Space Age."

First Moon Landing

Two years later, the Soviets also became the first to land a craft on the Moon. Luna 2 was a small spacecraft, only 3 feet (1 m) across, designed to crash-land on the lunar (Moon's) surface. Luna 2 was destroyed on impact, but it proved that a spacecraft could reach the Moon.

The V-2 rocket was first made by the Germans. The Americans quickly copied the design and made their own rocket weapons during the war.

Sputnik 1 launched our way of life today. There are now more than 10,000 active human-made satellites moving around Earth. They allow us to use devices such as cell phones and **GPS** systems. They also provide weather information.

Sputnik 1 sent out radio signals that gave scientists a lot of new information about Earth's atmosphere.

Before the Soviets launched Sputnik 1, the Americans had achieved their own "first" by sending a monkey, named Albert II, into space on a V-2 rocket. Albert II soared to 83 miles (134 km) above Earth's surface, but he did not survive the return journey. Experiments like this gave scientists an idea of how living creatures coped with being in space.

The Soviets were also experimenting with animals in space. Their second satellite, Sputnik 2, carried a passenger—a dog called Laika. She was the first animal to orbit Earth. Scientists did not yet know how to bring a spacecraft back once it was in orbit, so Laika died in space.

HAM, whose name was an acronym for Holloman Aero Med, became the first chimpanzee in space.

*"Nothing will stop us.
The road to the stars is steep and dangerous.
But we are not afraid....
Space flights can't be stopped."*

*Russian **cosmonaut***
Yuri Gagarin

Fighter pilot Yuri Gagarin's space flight took 108 minutes.

There is a monument to Laika in Moscow, Russia.

On April 12, 1961, Russian cosmonaut Yuri Gagarin made history—he became the first man in space. He made one orbit of Earth in Vostok 1, traveling at an incredible speed of 17,500 miles per hour (28,000 km/h)! Less than two hours after launch, Gagarin parachuted out of the spacecraft and drifted safely back to Earth.

Russian Valentina Tereshkova was the first woman in space. On June 16, 1963, she took off in a Vostok 6 spacecraft from the world's first space-launching facility, the Baikonur Cosmodrome. Tereshkova spent nearly three days in orbit, traveling over one million miles (1.6 million km). At the age of 70, Tereshkova said she would like to join a mission to Mars—even if it was a one-way trip!

Project Apollo

On May 25, 1961, President John F. Kennedy made a big announcement. He said that the U.S. would land a man on the Moon "before this decade is out." Kennedy was right. In July 1969, astronauts Neil Armstrong and Buzz Aldrin became the first humans to set foot on another world. But it was a long journey, in more ways than one.

In 1961, NASA announced its plan to begin a series of manned and unmanned missions to study the Moon. Unfortunately, this series of missions, called Project Apollo, got off to a tragic start. On January 27, 1967, during a practice mission, a fire broke out in the small **command module** of Apollo 1. The fire killed all three astronauts inside.

"We are going to have failures. There are going to be sacrifices made in the program. ...The [discovery] of space is worth the risk of life."

Virgil "Gus" Grissom, one of the three astronauts who died in Apollo 1

The astronauts of Apollo 1: Gus Grissom, Ed White, and Roger Chaffee.

After the terrible fate of Apollo 1, everyone was nervous about the next manned mission. But all went well with Apollo 7. This mission's goal was to orbit Earth and test the program's new command module. The astronauts also took a video camera with them. For the first time, people on Earth saw live pictures of astronauts floating in their spacecraft.

The Far Side

The next step in the program was to take the command module on an orbit of the Moon. In December 1968, Apollo 8 carried astronauts Jim Lovell, Bill Anders, and Frank Borman deeper into space than humans had ever been. Apollo 8 was the first time anyone had ever seen the far side of the Moon!

From Apollo 8 onward, Moon missions were launched using a Saturn V rocket. These were taller than a 35-story building and weighed more than 6 million pounds (3 million kg). Each of these massive rockets would cost more than $1 billion today.

The Apollo 8 crew included (L to R) Jim Lovell, Command Module (CM) pilot; Bill Anders, Lunar Module (LM) Pilot; and Frank Borman, Commander.

Apollo 11 on the Moon

July 20, 1969. After a three-day journey from Earth, the Apollo 11 lunar module Eagle touched down on a part of the Moon known as the Sea of Tranquility. Neil Armstrong climbed carefully down the ladder and stepped out onto the surface of the Moon. Buzz Aldrin followed him. In the command module, Michael Collins listened to the **transmissions** between his fellow astronauts and the excited team at Mission Control back on Earth.

Once on the surface, Armstrong and Aldrin took a telephone call from President Richard Nixon. Then they set about collecting samples of Moon rocks and dust. They also took plenty of photographs. After nearly a day on the surface, they climbed back into the Eagle and headed back to the command module. History had been made.

The lunar module was one of three parts that made up the Apollo 11 craft. There was also the service module and the command module, called Columbia. The command module was where the astronauts lived during their journey. It was the only part that returned to Earth.

Armstrong and Aldrin conducted scientific experiments and left a plaque on the Moon honoring the three Apollo 1 astronauts who had died.

The Apollo 13 astronauts are lifted to safety from the Odyssey command module after their splashdown.

Apollo 13

Apollo 13 was heading to the Moon to explore an area called the Fra Mauro Highlands. Two days into its journey, there was an explosion in one of the oxygen tanks, leaving the astronauts short on air. The tanks also ran the fuel cells that provided the electricity. Now they wouldn't have enough power for the return journey. Experts on the ground desperately tried to find a way to fix the damaged spacecraft. Then they had to get Apollo 13 home.

The astronauts guided the spacecraft around the Moon. They used its gravity to boost them homeward. Then they switched off everything they could to save as much power as possible. They survived for days in near-freezing conditions, but at last they made a safe splashdown in the Pacific Ocean.

NASA described Apollo 13 as a "successful failure." The astronauts did not reach the Moon, but they returned safely to Earth against all the odds.

Apollo 15

Apollo 15 was the ninth manned mission to the Moon. This was the first time that the special vehicle called the Lunar Roving Vehicle was used to explore the landscape of the Moon. The astronauts also carried out several **EVAs** (Extravehicular Activity) both from the surface of the Moon and in space.

In December 1972, the Apollo 17 astronauts became the last men to stand on the Moon. One of them, Harrison Schmitt, was the first professional scientist to go there. Over 50 years later, the Moon is once again being discussed as a possible refueling station for more distant exploration.

Apollo 17 was the first and only Moon mission to be launched at night.

"No single space project in this period will be more impressive to mankind, or more important for the long-range exploration of space."
U.S. President John F. Kennedy, talking about the Apollo missions

Powered by electricity, the Lunar Roving Vehicle had a top speed of 8 mph (13 km/h).

What's Next

While the Apollo missions were going on, NASA was also exploring other parts of the solar system. It used **probes** to find out more about the other planets, including the Pioneer probes. Pioneer probes were sent to Jupiter, Saturn, and Venus. They were even sent to the Sun.

Pioneers 10 and 11 were designed to travel farther than any other spacecraft had before. They journeyed to the part of space called the **asteroid** belt, which is an area between Mars and Jupiter, then on to the outer solar system. Scientists learned a lot from the information the Pioneers sent back, before they lost contact with Pioneer 11 in 1995 and Pioneer 10 in 2003.

This drawing shows Pioneer 10 reaching the planet Jupiter.

Pioneers 10 and 11 each carry a golden plaque. These show pictures of a man and a woman. They also explain where the space probes came from, in case they are found by other life-forms.

The Voyager Probes

The Voyager probes were launched in 1977. Their main mission was to send back information about the outer planets—Jupiter, Saturn, Uranus, and Neptune. The Voyagers showed scientists Saturn's rings in amazing detail. They also discovered that there were active volcanoes on Io, one of Jupiter's moons.

Both Voyager probes are still exploring the universe. They are both now in **interstellar** space, which is outside our solar system—around 12 billion miles (19 billion km) from our Sun. Both probes are still sending information home, although distance and age have begun to challenge communication from Voyager 1.

Space Shuttles

Until the 1980s, spacecraft could only be used for one mission. In 1983, NASA revealed the first reusable space vehicle—the Space Shuttle. They built a fleet of six shuttles that were designed to carry astronauts and supplies to and from Earth's orbit. Each shuttle could be used around 100 times. Powered by five massive rocket motors, they could travel at 17,000 miles per hour (27,500 km/h).

In January 1986, the shuttle *Challenger* was setting off on a routine mission. Just after launch, the fuel system failed. The shuttle exploded, killing all seven astronauts on board. Disaster struck again in 2003. The shuttle *Columbia* broke apart as it was coming back from a mission. Seven astronauts also died in this tragedy.

> *"They had a hunger to explore the universe and discover its truths. They wished to serve, and they did."*
>
> *President Ronald Reagan, talking about the* Challenger *astronauts*

The Space Shuttles looked more like airplanes than rockets.

Space Stations

A space station is a special kind of spacecraft. It is not designed for traveling into deep space. It is meant to stay in orbit around Earth. Scientists use space stations as research centers. The stations have laboratories and all the things astronauts need to live in space.

Assembly of the International Space Station (ISS) began in 1998. It was built in space, piece by piece. The first crew moved into the ISS in 2000. Astronauts from many different countries work together in the ISS to understand more about space.

NASA astronauts Jessica Watkins and Bob Hines work on the XROOTS space botany investigation on the International Space Station.

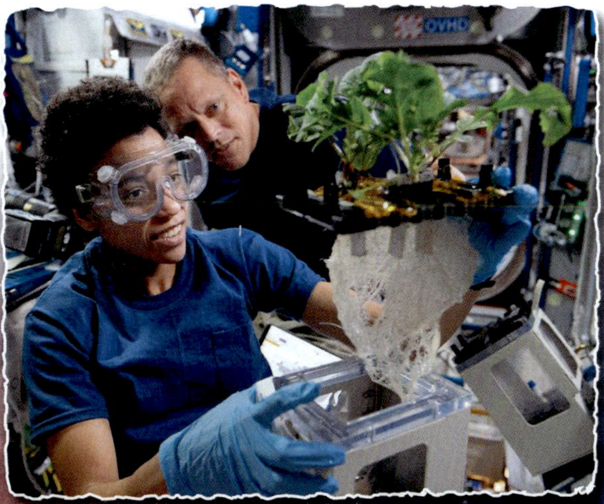

Mars and Beyond

We have put humans on the Moon. We have probed the outer planets. We have even sent spacecraft beyond our solar system. As technology continues to develop and our understanding of space grows, what might we discover next? How far will we travel?

The U.S. and Russia (the former USSR) are no longer the only countries with space agencies like NASA. The European Space Agency, as well as countries such as China, India, and Israel, all have space programs. Private companies are also starting to fund space exploration.

Two giant telescopes orbiting Earth can see deep into space. The Hubble and James Webb (above) space telescopes have taken incredible pictures of the creation of stars and of faraway galaxies.

Scientists can control the Mars rovers from Earth.

Is it possible to live on another planet? Scientists think it might be. Since the 1970s, spacecraft have been exploring Mars to see if it might support human life. The very first Mars mission was the Soviet probe Mars 2. It was built in two parts—one part to land on the planet and the other to orbit it.

In 2004, NASA landed two "rovers" on Mars. These robotic vehicles are called Spirit and Opportunity. They move around the surface of the planet, sending back information about the soil and any evidence of liquid water. Liquid water is the key to life. Ripples found in rock on the surface of Mars show that water had existed there in the past. The search continues to see if any water exists below the surface.

Today, Russian and European astronauts work alongside NASA astronauts on the ISS.

Life on Mars

No one has ever walked on Mars, but perhaps that could change. What would it take for humans to explore, and later live on, the planet? One of the biggest problems is how to protect astronauts from the radiation on Mars. But there are still many other challenges that humans will face.

Exploring Mars will be a tough mission. Astronauts will be away for years, not days like they were for the Moon missions. They will have to live in crowded conditions with the same small group of people. Astronauts on a mission like this will have to go through many tests to make sure they are up to the job!

A trip to Mars would likely take about nine months. NASA and other private space companies are trying to figure out how to make Mars **habitable** for humans. How can oxygen, water, and food be provided for a long stay?

There is barely any oxygen on Mars, and it has very low gravity. This means people living and working there will have to wear spacesuits outside.

Europa Mission

Mars might not be the only other place in space where people could live. NASA launched a probe called Europa Clipper in 2024 that should reach Jupiter's moon, Europa, by 2030. The plan is to find out if there might be liquid water beneath Europa's icy surface.

Landing on an Asteroid

Asteroids are space objects that give us a lot of useful information. In 2016, NASA sent a special unmanned spacecraft, called OSIRIS-REx, to collect samples of rock and dust from a nearby asteroid named Bennu. The analysis of the materials brought back in 2023 showed it contained elements needed to support life.

The European Space Agency sent a probe called Rosetta to **Comet** 67P/Churyumov–Gerasimenko. After 10 years, it arrived in 2014. The probe sent a small device to the surface of the comet, which sent back information to Earth.

Space Tourism

Space agencies such as NASA will continue to explore deep space, but private companies are now starting to fund near-Earth space transportation. This includes space tourism. In 2001, American millionaire Dennis Tito became the world's first space tourist. He trained for 900 hours and paid $20 million to spend six days on the International Space Station.

Soon, other people will have the chance to tour space. Private companies such as Virgin Galactic, Blue Origin, and SpaceX are accepting applications for future astronauts—if they have hundreds of thousands—sometimes millions—of dollars to spare! Perhaps within the next few decades, traveling beyond Earth will be as common as flying by airplane.

If there is water on the moon Europa, humans may one day be able to live there.

CHAPTER 3

Tanks

Beasts of the Battlefield

February 1991. U.S. troops had been traveling in tanks for days through the Iraqi desert. Outside, the rain poured violently. The passing sandstorms were blinding, and the tank drivers had no roads to follow. Instead, they found their way using GPS (Global Positioning System). No one had ever used this before.

Tanks have been used in warfare for over 100 years. The first tank was used on September 15, 1916.

The Battle of 73 Easting

On February 26, U.S. tanks finally arrived at a place in the desert known as 73 Easting. There, they braced themselves for battle against the Iraqi army, known as the Iraqi Republican Guard (IRG). The soldiers could hardly see because of a sandstorm. Thermal sights—devices that locate objects by the heat they give off—helped them find the enemy tanks. With the help of these new technologies, the U.S. only lost one tank at the end of the fierce battle.

Battle-Ready Tanks

Tanks, or armored fighting vehicles (AFVs), are combat vehicles protected by heavy armor. They can drive easily through the most difficult landscapes. Even terrible weather cannot stop them. Modern tanks have technology that helps soldiers find their way, or locate their enemies in fog or sandstorms.

Designing and building tanks with the best technology is a never-ending race. A country may make armor that will protect a tank from the deadliest **artillery**. But it is never long before another country develops weapons and ammunition, such as bullets and shells, that can damage that armor.

With their strong armor and modern weapons, tanks can be deadly on a battlefield.

Armored Fighting Vehicles

Tanks are built to carry out different jobs on the battlefield. The first tanks were grouped as heavy, medium, or light. The group they were in depended on their weight, gun size, amount of armor, and their purpose in battle. Later, heavy and medium tanks became known as main battle tanks (MBTs).

Light tanks include armored cars and fighting vehicles used by soldiers fighting on foot. Most light tanks have guns or cannons, but their main roles are to scout, or search, out dangerous areas or to carry large numbers of soldiers.

Fighting a Tank

Anti-tank guns are large guns or cannons that shoot ammunition that can stop a tank in its tracks. Some anti-tank guns are towed to the battlefield, while others are self-propelled, or able to move using their own engine. There are some anti-tank guns that look like tanks, but they do not have the same strong armor.

High-explosive anti-tank (HEAT) shells contain explosives with a copper lining in the tip of the bullet. Upon contact, the copper melts and the explosive pushes the shell through the tank's armor. A sabot is a narrow metal dart or arrow that sits inside a shell. The shell fills the large barrel of a gun but falls away from the dart after it is shot. HEAT and sabots can both injure or kill tank crews.

main battle gun: Mounted on the turret; shoots the heaviest ammunition

hull: The body of a tank that holds the engine, computer, crew members, and tracks

The gunner uses "sights" to target the enemy. These devices have night-vision so they can be used in the dark as well as daylight.

turret: A round armored weapon platform that holds the main gun or cannon and/or machine guns. It sits on top of a tank and rotates in a full circle.

Tank Crews

In a battle situation, most MBTs need at least four people to operate them. While **deployed**, crews may have to live inside their tank for days. The driver sits in a tiny, tight space at the front. He or she has to lean far back in the chair to fit. The commander works in the turret. Commanders communicate with other tanks and tell the crew what to do.

The gunner is in charge of firing the turret gun as well as the main battle gun. Laser range-finders help a gunner by using a laser beam to measure the distance to a target. Once the gunner pinpoints the target, he or she tells the loader what ammunition to put into the main gun.

caterpillar tracks: Metal linked treads turned by wheels

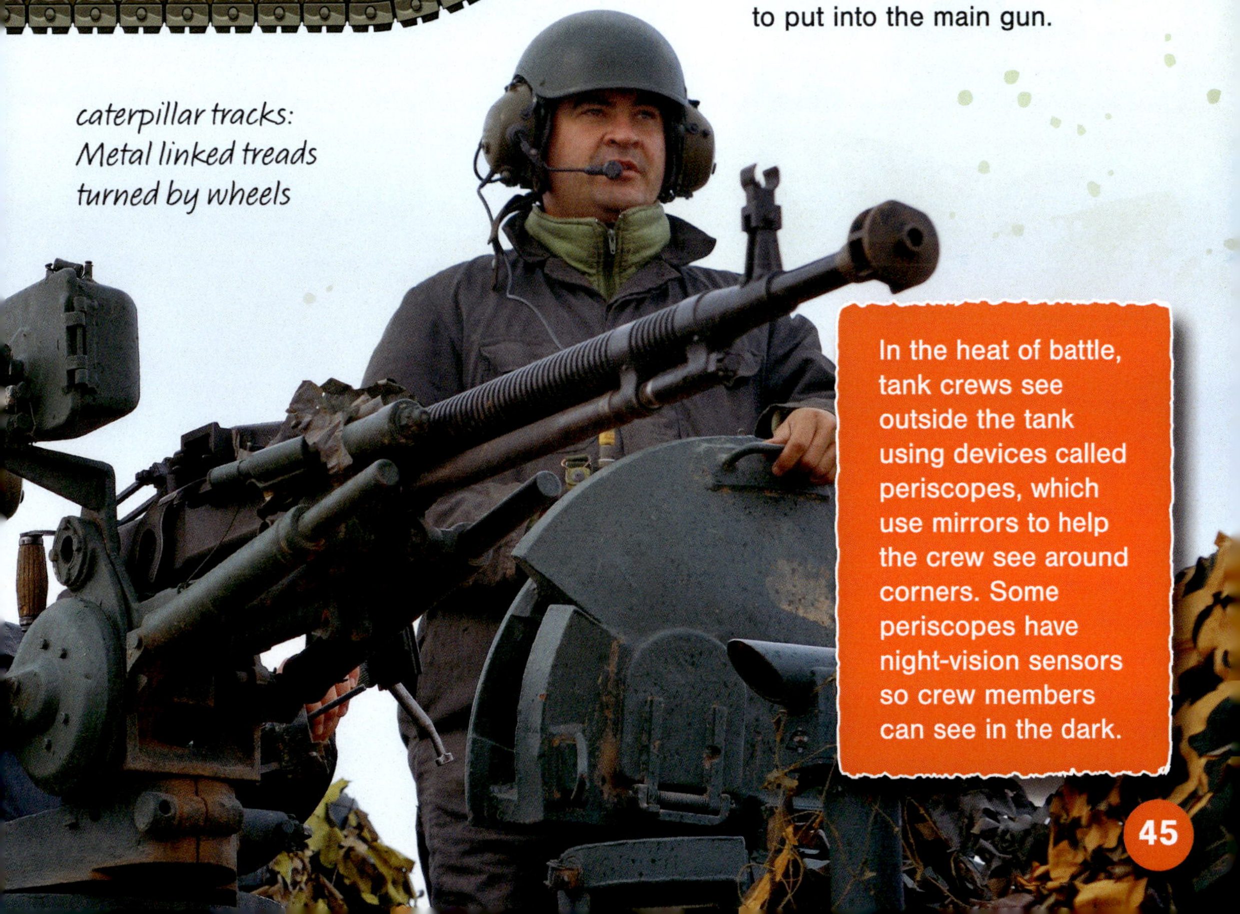

In the heat of battle, tank crews see outside the tank using devices called periscopes, which use mirrors to help the crew see around corners. Some periscopes have night-vision sensors so crew members can see in the dark.

Tanks in World War I

During World War I (1914–18), soldiers shot at their enemy from inside **trenches**. Barbed wire was placed in front of trenches to stop attacking soldiers from reaching them. Trench warfare resulted in long battles where many men were killed, but where no side gained land or victories.

The British called their Armored Fighting Vehicle a "water tank." This name threw off the enemy. They believed it was a tank used to hold water. The name "tank" stuck and is still used today.

The British wanted to break the **stalemate**. Their navy began designing and building an armed and armored vehicle that would help British soldiers attack enemy trenches. In 1916, they revealed the result—a type of "land ship" that ran on tracks. One hundred of these tanks were built. They became known as the Mark I.

The Battle of the Somme

In 1916, the **Allies** launched an attack at the Somme, France, where their German enemies had created a strong system of trenches. The Battle of the Somme lasted many months. Thousands of Allied soldiers died every day. Still, they could not defeat the Germans. The British decided to unleash their secret weapon.

On September 15, 1916, 15 British tanks went roaring onto the battlefield for the first time. No one had seen anything like the tanks before. German soldiers panicked at the sight of them. But despite their new weapon, the Allies gained only 1 mile (1.6 km) of land. Many tanks were caught in ditches, broke down, or were stopped by artillery fire.

Britain's new secret weapon had to drive through mud and over rocks and large potholes while protecting soldiers. The earliest designs were armed with large guns and machine guns that shot bullets continuously.

The Battle of Cambrai

The Germans also held a strong trench system in another part of France called Cambrai. The Allies planned to use tanks to defeat the enemy there, but they were worried that the tanks would not be able to cross the trenches. To solve this problem, some tanks carried bundles of wood to drop in the trenches. This would help the tanks cross over into battle.

More than 400 tanks were secretly brought to Cambrai. Early in the morning of November 20, 1917, soldiers began laying out the bridges. The plan worked perfectly. With the help of tanks, the Allies **advanced** about 5 miles (8 km) and captured around 8,000 German soldiers.

The only tanks that Germany made during World War I were around 20 A7V tanks. The first German tank was used in battle in March 1918. It carried one main gun and six machine guns.

The tanks used in the Battle of Cambrai were Mark IVs, which had much stronger armor than earlier versions.

The Battle of Amiens

The Battle of Amiens was the largest tank battle of World War I. The Allies secretly brought in more than 600 tanks before the battle began. Some of these were the new British Mark V tanks. They had more powerful engines and better tracks. The hull was designed with slits so the crew could see better. Another gun was added to the rear.

The surprise attack at Amiens began on August 8, 1918. Tanks led the way and protected the **infantry** soldiers following behind. Tanks shot and killed enemy machine-gunners. More than 20,000 German soldiers died. The Germans called the first day of the Battle of Amiens "Black Day." This defeat was the turning point in the war.

The German A7V tanks could each hold up to 18 soldiers.

Tanks in World War II

Tanks became even more important in World War II (1939–45). This war began in September 1939, when the German leader Adolf Hitler ordered the invasion of Poland. The Germans used the combined **tactics** of speed and surprise in their invasion. This became known as "Blitzkrieg," which means "lightning war."

German armored tank units—called Panzer divisions—played a new role in warfare. The Panzer MBTs quickly broke through weak enemy lines, with support from artillery and attacks from aircraft. The Germans used Blitzkrieg successfully against other European countries in the first few years of World War II.

The Allies produced thousands more tanks than the **Axis powers** in World War II. These included 84,000 Russian-made T-34s. At the beginning of World War II, the T-34 was the best tank on the battlefield. In 1942, Germany created two new types of tanks, called Tiger and Panther, which were a deadly threat to the Allies. However, Germany could not build enough of them.

El Alamein

Germany's Panzer divisions were winning the battles in North Africa, but they were running low on fuel and ammunition. The Allies used this to their advantage. During the Second Battle of El Alamein in Egypt, they used more than 800 tanks against the Germans. The Germans had around 400 tanks, but within a few weeks only 20 were left fighting. The Germans were soon forced to retreat.

The T-34 design remained in service for over 20 years—longer than any other tank.

*"Today we are crushed by the sheer weight of the **mechanized** forces hurled against us, but we can still look to a future in which even greater mechanized force will bring us victory."*

French General Charles de Gaulle, after the Germans invaded France, in 1940

The Battle of Kursk

The biggest tank battle of World War II was the Battle of Kursk. By 1943, the Russian, then called Soviet, army had formed a strong line of defense around the Russian city of Kursk. On July 5, Germany attacked Kursk with thousands of tanks at both ends of the line. But the Soviets had many more tanks—they were ready to fight back!

As the German tanks began gaining ground toward Kursk, the Russian 5th Guards Tank Army set out to face them. The two sides met near the Russian city of Prokhorovka. The Soviets started with more tanks, but they also lost more than the Germans in the battle. Despite this, on August 23, the German army finally gave up and retreated. The Allies had won.

Amphibious tanks were first used for warfare during World War II. Some were used during the D-Day landings in 1944, when Allied forces launched a surprise attack on the Germans at Normandy, France, after crossing the English Channel.

The Allied tanks at El Alamein included the mighty American Sherman tanks.

> "Wittman was a Nazi [German] from the start. It didn't matter who killed him, just that he was killed."
>
> British tank gunner Joe Ekins, reported to have killed German tank commander Michael Wittman

German Tank Aces

A tank ace is a hero who "kills" or destroys the most tanks during a war. German tank ace Kurt Knispel was a loader, gunner, and tank commander. He was World War II's ace of aces with 168 Allied tank kills. Tank commander Michael Wittman was another famous German tank ace. On one occasion, he destroyed 14 Allied tanks in 15 minutes.

Allied Aces

Soviet tank commander Dmitry Lavrinenko was the Allied tank ace of aces in World War II. He had over 50 tank kills in his T-34. Canadian tank ace Sydney Valpy Radley-Walters—known as "Captain Rad"—figured out that there was a weak spot at the base of the turret on the German Tiger tank. This information helped other Allied tank crews destroy German tanks.

Tanks in Modern Conflicts

Between 1954 and 1975, North and South Vietnam were at war. The U.S. joined forces with South Vietnam. American troops used the newly designed M48 Patton tanks as MBTs. The turret and hull had stronger, cast steel armor. The turret was curved, which gave better protection. The M48 came with a larger gun.

On January 31, 1968, North Vietnam invaded the city of Hue, South Vietnam. This began the longest and bloodiest battle of the Vietnam War. Once inside the city walls, **snipers** and machine-gunners hid in buildings and began firing on the South Vietnamese. American armored tanks, including M113 armored personnel carriers (APCs), were used to help drive the North Vietnamese back.

The U.S. Marines used M48 Patton medium tanks during the Vietnam War.

A Syrian T-55 and Israeli Centurion tank stand as a memorial to the battle in the Valley of Tears.

After the Yom Kippur War, the Israelis named the valley at Golan Heights the "Valley of Tears" because of all the soldiers who died in the battle there.

The Yom Kippur War

In October 1973, a **coalition** that included Egypt and Syria launched a surprise attack on Israel during their religious holiday of Yom Kippur. They hoped to force Israel to leave the areas of Sinai and Golan Heights in the Middle East. The coalition had many more tanks, artillery, and soldiers than the Israeli army.

At Golan Heights, less than 200 Israeli Centurion tanks positioned on top of a hill were outnumbered by about 1,000 Syrian T-62 tanks in the valley below. The battle went on until only seven Israeli tanks remained. Thirteen damaged Israeli tanks operated by injured Israeli soldiers came to their rescue. They helped Israel win the battle.

The Gulf War

In August 1990, Iraqi leader Saddam Hussein ordered his army to invade Kuwait. Thousands of Iraqi tanks **spearheaded** the invasion, including Soviet-made tanks such as the T-72. The U.S., Britain, and 27 other countries formed a coalition to stop Iraq. This marked the start of the First Gulf War.

Over 1,800 American M1A1 Abrams MBTs joined the coalition fight in the Iraqi desert, known as Operation Desert Storm. Their large guns were able to shoot distances of over 1.5 miles (2.4 km). This was about half a mile (0.8 km) farther than the Iraqi tank guns could shoot. These powerful tanks helped the U.S. and its allies defeat Iraqi forces in 100 hours.

The M1A1 Abrams tank had serious firepower and could travel at up to 42 miles per hour (68 km/h).

"The turrets were flipping 40...50 feet in the air. [...] It was incredible to see a gun tube and the turret just spinning up in the air and landing hundreds of yards away from the (tanks)."

U.S. Sergeant John Scaglione, describing an Iraqi tank being destroyed

Bradley Fighting Vehicles are special armored vehicles used for transporting infantry soldiers during battle.

Tactical internet is a secure communications system that cannot be jammed by the enemy. In the Gulf War, it allowed coalition forces to talk to one another safely.

Second Gulf War

In March 2003, a coalition of countries including the U.S. and Britain went to war with Iraq again. This time, they hoped to rid the country of Saddam Hussein's government. The U.S. claimed the Iraqis had nuclear bombs, which made them a dangerous enemy. The **campaign**—known as Operation Iraqi Freedom—began with air bombings. These were quickly followed by a ground invasion spearheaded by tanks.

In April, coalition forces invaded Iraq's capital city, Baghdad. The armored attack on Baghdad, called Operation Thunder Run, included M1A1 Abrams MBTs and Bradley Fighting Vehicles. Heat exhaustion was a big risk for crews inside these vehicles. Temperatures in the tanks reached more than 100 °Fahrenheit (38 °C).

The South Ossetia War

The state of South Ossetia declared its independence from the country of Georgia in August 2008. This sparked a five-day battle between them. Georgian tanks, including T-72 MBTs, attacked the city of Tskhinvali in South Ossetia. Russia set up a military compound—a protected area that contains buildings—there to help the South Ossetians.

There was fierce fighting between the Georgian and Russian tanks. Three Russian BMP-1s were destroyed, killing all their crew members. The Russians fired back with a rocket-propelled grenade. This is a powerful form of ammunition launched by a rocket. It destroyed one of the T-72s. The conflict ended a few days later, when the Georgian army withdrew.

Shockwaves are violent forces of energy from explosions. They often cause the most damage to tanks. A shockwave passing through a tank can harm the structure, systems, and crew inside.

LAV IIIs are wheeled armored vehicles that have run-flat tires. These are special tires that can travel for miles even if they have been punctured.

The Future of Tanks

Today, soldiers are often sent to countries for peacekeeping duties. Tanks with caterpillar tracks are heavy, expensive to transport, and travel slowly. They can ruin roads. Seeing tanks rolling through their towns and villages can scare **civilians**. For all these reasons, wheeled armored vehicles are used more often than tanks in peacekeeping missions.

Light armored vehicles (LAVs) such as the Stryker (U.S.) or LAV III (Canada) are armored vehicles with six, eight, or 12 wheels. They send power to each wheel separately, which helps them drive over almost any surface. They can travel at speeds of up to 60 miles per hour (100 km/h).

Future Fights

Modern conflicts are global and often arise quickly. Countries need to be able to **mobilize** a combat force at any time, and place it around the world within a few days. Armored vehicles, such as tanks, may need to be transported to a battleground by air. The great weight of tanks makes this difficult.

In 2009, the U.S. Army canceled its Future Combat Systems (FCS) program. This had planned to design lighter armored vehicles so the army could mobilize easier and faster. U.S. military leaders scrapped the project because they felt their troops needed the heavy-armor protection of MBTs.

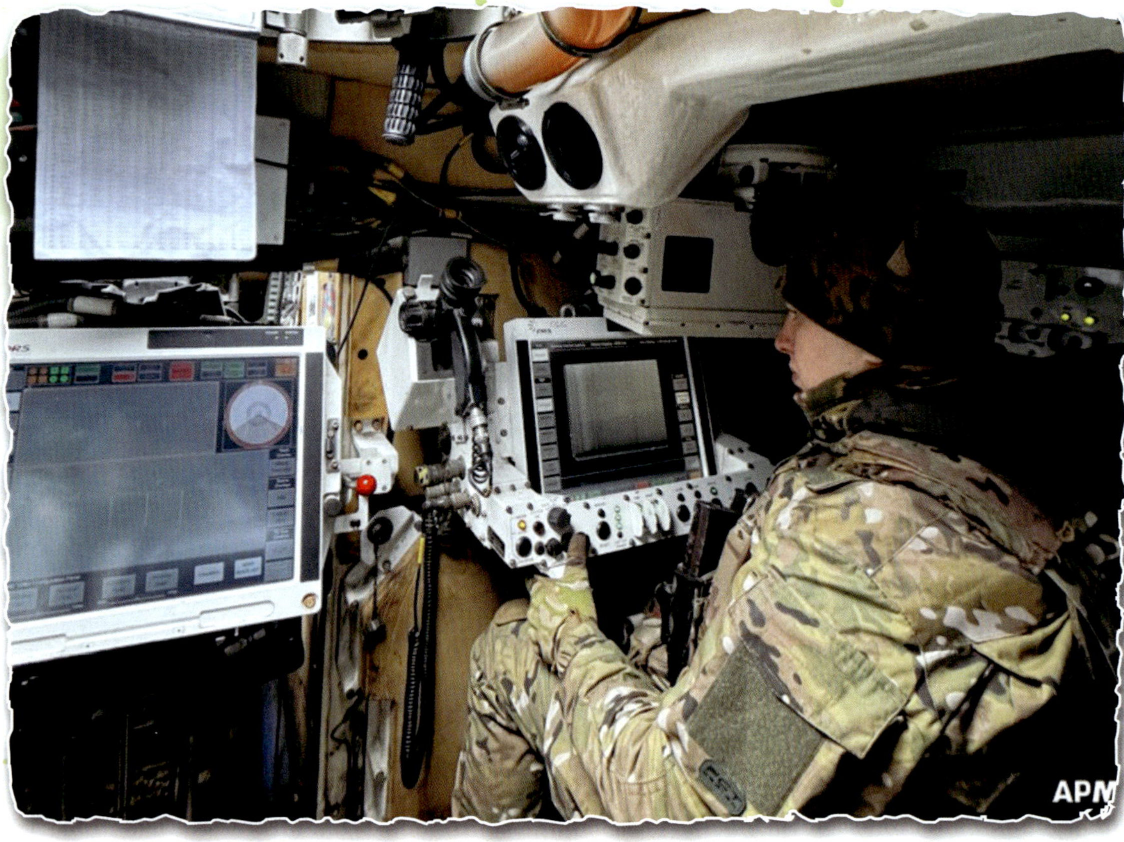
APM

Today's modern conflicts often involve smaller rebel groups fighting against a government. These conflicts are fought with weapons such as roadside bombs and rocket-propelled guns. The heavy armor of MBTs offers the best protection against these kinds of weapons.

New technology allows tank commanders to know exactly where their allies—and their enemies—are on the battlefield.

ADAPTIV is technology that allows a tank to hide from its enemies. It can change the temperature of a tank to confuse enemy heat-seeking missiles.

The South Korean K2 Black Panther is one of the most advanced tanks in the world today.

Future Tank-nology

Tanks are expensive to build—one M1 Abrams tank costs up to $10 million! For this reason, most countries **upgrade** their tanks with new technologies instead of replacing them. Engineers create better technologies to make MBTs faster, safer, and deadlier to the enemy.

Think-Tanks

Smart Armor is tank armor that has special built-in sensors that figure out what kind of ammunition it is being hit with. It also knows how much damage has been done to the tank. Many tanks also now have computer systems with Wireless Tactical Internet. This works with GPS and can share information with up to 1,000 military computers.

GLOSSARY

advanced Moved forward

Allies Countries, including Britain, France, United States, Russia, and Canada, that joined together to fight against the Axis powers in World War II

amphibious Made to work on or in water

artillery Large weapons that can shoot long distances

asteroid A rocky body, smaller than a planet, orbiting the Sun

atmosphere The gases that surround a planet

automaton (plural: automata) A moving machine, often in the shape of a human

autonomous Able to act independently

Axis powers The combined forces of Germany, Italy, and Japan in World War II

booby-trapped Set with a trap, such as a bomb or explosive device

campaign A series of battles planned to achieve victory in war

CapCom (Capsule Communicator) The person on Earth in charge of talking to astronauts in space

civilians People who do not belong to the armed forces

coalition A group of countries that join military forces

coexist To live alongside each other

comet A body of ice and dust in orbit in space

command module The control center and living quarters in a spacecraft

cosmonaut A Russian astronaut

deployed When soldiers are sent to do a particular job

digestive system The part of the body that breaks down food

eclipses Events in which an object in space blocks the light from another object, such as the Moon blocking the Sun

EVAs (extravehicular activities) When astronauts move around in space outside their spacecraft

GPS (Global Positioning System) A system that uses signals from satellites in space to determine locations

gravity The force of attraction between two objects

habitable Capable of being lived in

humanoid A robot with a human-like body

industrial Made in a factory

infantry Soldiers on foot

interstellar Among the stars, beyond our solar system

mechanized Powered by machinery

mobilize To get an army ready for war

orbited Moved around a circular object, such as Earth

paratroopers Soldiers trained to parachute from an airplane

probes Small, unmanned spacecraft

radiation A type of energy that can be harmful to people

reconnaissance A mission taken to find information about an enemy

robotic Describing a machine that can be programmed to do certain tasks

rover A vehicle for exploring the surface of a body in space

satellite A device that moves around Earth, collecting or sending information

sensors Devices that recognize something by one of the five senses

snipers Skilled shooters who work from a hidden position

spearheaded Led an attack

stalemate An outcome with no winner

stationary Staying in one place

tactics The way that a battle is carried out

tracks A moving track of metal links on which a tank's wheels ride

transmissions Radio messages

trenches Ditches dug in the ground in which soldiers shelter from enemy fire during battle

upgrade To improve a thing or replace with something better

LEARNING MORE

Books

Goldstein, Margaret J. *Investigating Mars.* Lerner Publishing Group, 2024.

Jackson, Tom. *Robot Obstacle Courses.* Lerner Publishing Group, 2025.

Klatte, Kathleen A. *Jobs in the U.S. Space Force.* Rosen Young Adult, 2022.

Oxlade, Chris. *Inside Tanks and Heavy Artillery.* Hungry Tomato, 2017.

Potter, William. *Robots.* Gareth Stevens, 2022.

West, David. *Tanks.* Crabtree Publishing, 2020.

Websites

https://science.nasa.gov/mission/msl-curiosity/
Learn about Mars through the robotic rover Curiosity.

www.pbs.org/wgbh/nova/robots/
A PBS site that explores future robots, dangerous-duty robots, and videos of robots in action.

http://mars.nasa.gov/participate/funzone/
See images taken of the red planet by rovers on NASA's Mars Exploration pages.

https://www.space.com/missions
A website with articles about all of NASA's past missions and current exploration in space.

www.tankmuseum.org
The Tank Museum website, with photographs, war stories, virtual tank museum, and more.

www.tanks-encyclopedia.com
Lists tanks by wars and countries.

INDEX